D0988785

123
SESAME STREET

Go Green with Sesame Street

FIGHT POLLUTION, BIG BIRD!

PALM BEACH COUNTY
LIBRARY SYSTEM
3650 Summit Boulevard
West Palm Beach, FL 33406-4198

Jennifer Boothroyd

Lerner Publications · Minneapolis

Cooperating and sharing are an important part of *Sesame Street*—and of taking care of our planet. We all share Earth, so it's up to all of us to take care of it together. The *Go Green with Sesame Street*® books cover everything from appreciating Earth's beauty, to conserving its resources, to helping keep it clean, and more. And the familiar, furry friends from *Sesame Street* offer young readers some easy ways to help protect their planet.

Sincerely,

The Editors at Sesame Workshop

The text of this book is printed on paper that is made with 30 percent recycled postconsumer waste fibers.

Table of Contents

Awesome Earth!

Wow! What an amazing and awesome planet we live on!

Earth Is Important

People live all around the world. Millions of different kinds of plants and animals live on Earth too.

Earth is big enough for everyone.

Earth gives us what we need to live and grow.

Plants are awesome. When Earth is healthy, plants, trees, and flowers grow.

This tree is thousands of years old.

Some plants make food for people and animals.

Me love blueberries!

Animals are awesome. When Earth is healthy, animals are healthy too.

This giraffe is taller than me!

Ants are tiny. But they can carry things that are *way* heavier than their own bodies.

All living things need clean water. People and animals drink water. Plants need water to grow.

All living things need air. People and animals need air to breathe. Plants need air to grow.

What Is Pollution?

Pollution is anything that makes the air, water, or land dirty.

I love trash, but it belongs in my can.

Some people leave trash on the ground. That trash is called litter.

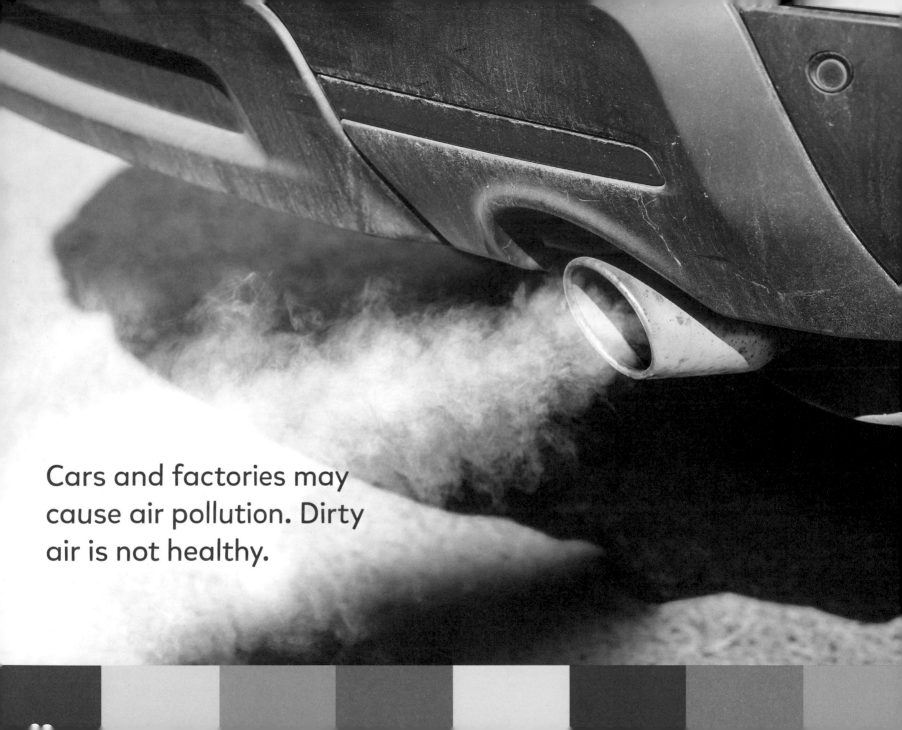

Cars and factories may cause air pollution. Dirty air is not healthy.

Sometimes garbage gets into the water.
Water pollution can make living things sick.

Keep Earth Clean

Respect Earth. Don't waste the things it gives us. Help protect our planet.

Earth gives us air to breathe, water to drink, and beautiful places to make homes.

We can give Earth something too.
We can take care of it.

Let's work together
to keep Earth clean!

Earth Day Every Day

Earth Day is April 22. People all around the world celebrate Earth on Earth Day.

People think about all the ways to help fight pollution. Sometimes they clean up litter on this day to help keep Earth clean and beautiful.

Plant It!

Plants can clean the air. Ask an adult to help you grow something amazing.

1. Find a spot for your plant. You will need a place with sunlight and good soil. If your plant is inside, you will need some dirt and a pot.

2. Dig a hole. Put your seeds or plant in the dirt. Cover up the rest of the hole.

3. Water your plant.

4. Watch your plant grow. Nature is so cool!

Glossary

factories: buildings where things are made

litter: trash that is left on the ground

pollution: something that makes the air, water, or land dirty

respect: to treat something in a nice way

Index

Photo Acknowledgments

Additional image credits: vectortatu/Shutterstock.com, throughout (background); Evgeni Dinev Photography/Getty Images, p. 5; FatCamera/Getty Images, p. 6; Jasper Cole/Getty Images, p. 7; SeventyFour/Getty Images, p. 8; Chiara Salvadori/Getty Images, p. 10; GomezDavid/Getty Images, p. 11; paulbanton/Getty Images, p. 12; dikkyoesin1/Getty Images, p. 13; RUNSTUDIO/Getty Images, p. 14; Vlad61/Shutterstock.com, p. 15; Jose Luis Pelaez Inc/Getty Images, p. 16; Linas Toleikis/Getty Images, p. 17; Roberto Macagnino/EyeEm/Getty Images, p. 19; ByoungJoo/Getty Images, p. 20; baona/Getty Images, p. 21; Hero Images/Getty Images, pp. 22, 26; Paul Sutherland Photography/Getty Images, p. 23; Ariel Skelley/Getty Images, pp. 24, 28; Caiaimage/Trevor Adeiline/Getty Images, p. 28; Emily Suzanne McDonald/Getty Images, p. 30.
Cover: Yuri Parmenov/Getty Images (dots), vectortatu/Shutterstock.com (background).

Copyright © 2020 Sesame Workshop.® Sesame Street.® and associated characters, trademarks and design elements are owned and licensed by Sesame Workshop. All rights reserved.

International copyright secured. No part of this book may be reproduced, stored in a retrieval system, or transmitted in any form or by any means—electronic, mechanical, photocopying, recording, or otherwise—without the prior written permission of Lerner Publishing Group, Inc., except for the inclusion of brief quotations in an acknowledged review.

Lerner Publications Company
An imprint of Lerner Publishing Group, Inc.
241 First Avenue North
Minneapolis, MN 55401 USA

For reading levels and more information, look up this title at www.lernerbooks.com.

Main body text set in Mikado. Typeface provided by HVD.

Library of Congress Cataloging-in-Publication Data

Names: Boothroyd, Jennifer, 1972- author.
Title: Fight pollution, Big Bird! / Jennifer Boothroyd.
Description: Minneapolis, MN, USA : Lerner Publications, [2020] | Series: Go green with Sesame Street | Audience: Age 4–8. | Audience: K to Grade 3. | Includes bibliographical references.
Identifiers: LCCN 2019010647 (print) | LCCN 2019018499 (ebook) | ISBN 9781541583108 (eb pdf) | ISBN 9781541572614 (lib. bdg.)
Subjects: LCSH: Pollution—Juvenile literature. | Pollution prevention—Juvenile literature.
Classification: LCC TD176 (ebook) | LCC TD176 .B66 2020 (print) | DDC 363.73—dc23

LC record available at https://lccn.loc.gov/2019010647

Manufactured in the United States of America
1-46528-47573-8/7/2019